The SPORTS CLUB

Football

Jason Page

Published by Two-Can Publishing,
43-45 Dorset Street, London W1H 4AB

www.two-canpublishing.com

© Two-Can Publishing 2000

For information on Two-Can books and multimedia, call
(0)20 7224 2440, fax (0)20 7224 7005, or visit our website at
http://www.two-canpublishing.com

Created by
act-two
346 Old Street
London EC1V 9RB

Text: Jason Page
Editor: Jacqueline McCann
Assistant editor: Lucy Arnold
Art director: Belinda Webster
Designers: Helen Holmes and Joanna Pocock
Consultant: Shaun Gore, Football in the Community,
  Chelsea Football Club, London
Computer generated figures: Jonatronix
Computer illustrations: Mel Pickering
Picture research: Jenny West
Production: Adam Wilde

'Two-Can' is a trademark of Two-Can Publishing Ltd
Two-Can Publishing is a division of Zenith Entertainment plc,
43-45 Dorset Street, London W1H 4AB.

Hardback ISBN 1-85434-640-7
Paperback ISBN 1-85434-641-5

Dewey Decimal Classification 796.334

Hardback 10 9 8 7 6 5 4 3 2 1
Paperback 10 9 8 7 6 5 4 3 2 1

A catalogue record for this book is available from the British Library.

Photographic credits: Action Images p12, p14, p16, p24, p26, p27, p29
(bottom left); Allsport p5, p18, p19, p20, p29 (bottom right); Colorsport p22,
p28 (bottom), p29 (top); Empics p10, p28 (top); Popperfoto p8; PA News p21

Cover: Allsport (top left and bottom); Colorsport (top right)

Printed in Hong Kong by Wing King Tong

Contents

Words in **bold** in the text are explained here, along with other useful football terms.

Getting started

66 Hi, I'm your coach and it's my job to help you master the basic skills you need to play football — the world's most popular game! All you need is an open space, a ball and some friends and you're ready to start training. 99

What you need

All the players in a team wear the same-coloured kit, called a strip, to show they are on the same side. Often, players have numbers printed on the backs of their strips. For outdoor games, you need boots with studs that grip the **pitch**, and a football!

Check your studs before each game to make sure that they're not worn down.

Choose a football that is right for your size.

Shin pads protect the fronts of your legs.

Long socks help to hold the shin pads in place.

Warming up

A good warm-up is essential before a game. Always loosen up and stretch your muscles to avoid a painful injury. First, jog around the pitch or skip for a few minutes, then try these simple thigh and ankle exercises. End with a short sprint and you'll be ready to start playing. To pick up tips, watch how other teams warm up before a game!

To stretch your thigh, hold your ankle and gently pull it towards your buttocks. Count to five, then relax. Now stretch your other leg.

To exercise your ankle, stretch one leg out in front of you. Roll your foot around in a circle while you count to ten. Do the same with your other foot.

Juggling fun

Now that you've warmed up, practise controlling the ball. See how long you can keep the ball in the air using only your feet, thighs, head and chest. Why not ask a friend to time you? Try not to touch the ball with your arms or hands because this isn't allowed in football.

Practise short kick-ups. Lean back and bend your knees a little. Drop the ball on to your foot and kick it firmly with the top of your boot ten times.

Now bounce the ball with your thigh. When you can bounce the ball ten times in a row, try keeping the ball in the air using your head and chest.

Kicking the ball

Before a game, practise **passing** the ball back and forth with a team-mate. Start by kicking the ball with the inside of your foot. Then vary your technique by using other parts of your foot. This will help you to get a feel for the ball.

inside of foot · instep · sole · outside of foot

The safest way to kick the ball is with the inside of your foot, not with your toes. Aim for the middle of the ball to keep it low in the air.

By using different parts of your foot you can control the ball, or make it go in different directions. Use the inside, outside, instep and sole of your foot.

◄ Good team spirit helps you to play well and enjoy yourself at the same time. Practise the skills and tactics in this book and you'll be able to play a great team game with your friends.

HOT TIPS
Don't be afraid of the ball – get used to it and have confidence in your own ability.

Meet the team

Ben
Liz

" A football team is made up of 11 players. There are four main positions you can play – **striker**, **midfielder**, **defender** or **goalkeeper**. It's a coach's job to decide the way the players are arranged on the **pitch**. This is called the **formation**. **"**

Strikers

It's our job to score goals against the opposition. Strikers need to be speedy sprinters who can out-run the other team's defence and get into a good position to **shoot**. We must be deadly accurate and able to shoot with both feet.

Team formation

A coach may decide to make his team more attacking, by using more players as strikers. He may decide to play a more defensive game, by using more defenders. The most common formation uses four defenders, four midfielders and two strikers, so it's known as the 4-4-2 formation.

▶ It's the start of the match and the blue team is in its own half. The players are in a 4-4-2 formation. This line-up shows a good balance between attack and defence.

Attack
Two strikers stay forward. They rarely come back deep into their own half.

Ben
striker

Kim
midfielder

Raj
midfielder

Sue
defender

Jon
defender

Julie
goalkeeper

Left pitch
Players on the left-hand side of the pitch usually prefer to kick with their left feet.

Guarding the goal
The goalkeeper stays close to the goal. She must be alert and on guard at all times.

Midfielders

It's up to us to feed the ball to the strikers, or take a shot ourselves! If we lose possession of the ball, we race back to defend our own half, so we have to be really fit.

Defenders

Our job is to stop the opposition from moving forwards and shooting at the goal. We **tackle** opponents to win the ball, or kick it away to safety.

Raj

Kim

Dan

Matt

Jon

Tom

Sue

Sean

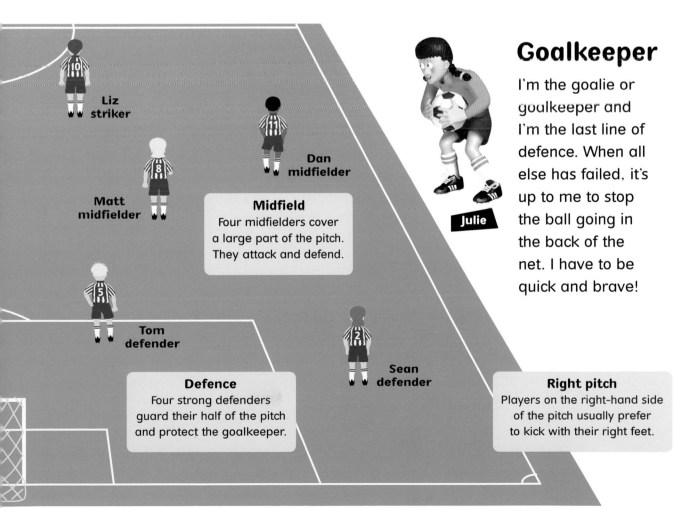

Liz
striker

Matt
midfielder

Dan
midfielder

Midfield
Four midfielders cover a large part of the pitch. They attack and defend.

Tom
defender

Sean
defender

Defence
Four strong defenders guard their half of the pitch and protect the goalkeeper.

Goalkeeper

I'm the goalie or goalkeeper and I'm the last line of defence. When all else has failed, it's up to me to stop the ball going in the back of the net. I have to be quick and brave!

Julie

Right pitch
Players on the right-hand side of the pitch usually prefer to kick with their right feet.

The rules

❝ I'm the **referee**, but call me Ref for short. If a player breaks the rules, he commits a **foul** and I blow my whistle to stop the game. I may award a **free kick**, or show a yellow card as a warning. A red card means you're off – I'm the one in charge on the **pitch**! **❞**

▲ During the 1998 **World Cup**, the England **midfielder** David Beckham was shown the red card.

The pitch

The aim of the game is to knock the ball into the other side's goal net, as many times as possible. A match lasts for 90 minutes, but after 45 minutes, there's a break called **half-time**. All the action takes place on a grassy pitch. Let's take a look...

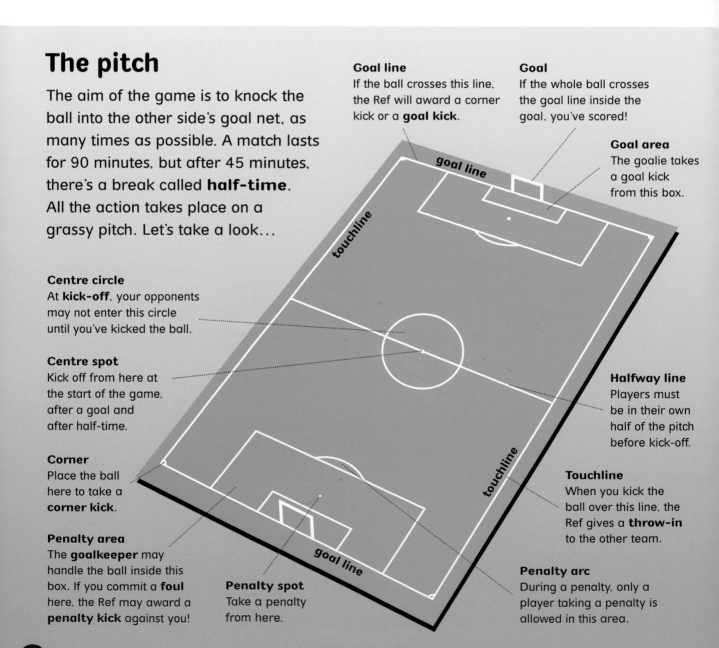

Goal line
If the ball crosses this line, the Ref will award a corner kick or a **goal kick**.

Goal
If the whole ball crosses the goal line inside the goal, you've scored!

Goal area
The goalie takes a goal kick from this box.

Centre circle
At **kick-off**, your opponents may not enter this circle until you've kicked the ball.

Centre spot
Kick off from here at the start of the game, after a goal and after half-time.

Corner
Place the ball here to take a **corner kick**.

Penalty area
The **goalkeeper** may handle the ball inside this box. If you commit a **foul** here, the Ref may award a **penalty kick** against you!

Penalty spot
Take a penalty from here.

Halfway line
Players must be in their own half of the pitch before kick-off.

Touchline
When you kick the ball over this line, the Ref gives a **throw-in** to the other team.

Penalty arc
During a penalty, only a player taking a penalty is allowed in this area.

goal line
touchline
touchline
goal line

Fouls and free kicks

What is a foul?

1 A **tackle** where you touch your opponent before you touch the ball
2 pushing, kicking or holding on to your opponent
3 tackling from behind
4 touching the ball with your arms or hands
5 **obstruction** – getting in your opponent's way.

What happens next?

If you commit a foul accidentally, the Ref awards an **indirect free kick** to the other team. If the Ref thinks that the foul was deliberate, he gives a **direct free kick**.

Indirect free kick

The ball bounces higher than Sean was expecting and it's a **hand-ball**! The Ref awards an indirect free kick to the other team.

Direct free kick

As Raj sprints with the ball, a red **defender** deliberately tackles him from behind. The Ref gives a direct free kick to Raj's team.

The red team takes the indirect free kick. They must pass the ball at least once before they can take a shot. It's a goal!

Liz takes the direct free kick for her team. She shoots straight at the goal – and scores! Well done, Liz!

Offside rule

When a team-mate behind you **passes** the ball forwards, there must be at least two opposition players level with, or between, you and the goal. Otherwise, you're **offside** and the Ref will give the other team a free kick.

This rule doesn't count if:

1 you are in your own half
2 you are behind the ball
3 you receive the ball from a throw-in, a corner kick or a goal kick.

❶ Dan wants to pass the ball forwards. Liz is **onside** because the red defender and goalie are in front of her.

❷ Ben is offside. There is only one opponent (the goalie) between him and the goal.

❸ If Dan kicks the ball forwards now, the Ref will stop play because Ben is offside.

The solution Ben should run back so that he's behind the red defender. Then Dan can pass the ball without breaking the rules.

Liz

Dan

Ben

Dribbling and turning

66 Now it's time to improve your skills. Let's start with **dribbling**, that's soccer-speak for running with the ball! Once you've mastered the basics, you'll be able to run rings around the opposition. 99

▲ The England striker Michael Owen is very fast and skilful at running past defenders with the ball.

Basic dribbling

The secret of good dribbling is not to kick the ball too hard — it should never be more than one step in front of you. Follow the ball, tapping it forwards with the sides of your feet. Remember that if you can't reach the ball, you can't control it.

Kim uses both the inside and outside edges of her boots to control the ball. She keeps her body over the ball and looks out for team-mates who are free.

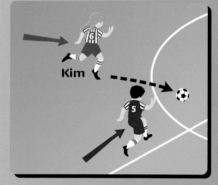

Kim needs more dribbling practice. She has kicked the ball too far ahead of her, making it easy for her opponent to steal it.

Stop turn

A great way to escape from an opposition player when you're dribbling is to change direction suddenly. Here's how it's done! Hop over the ball, then stop it using the heel or sole of your boot. Quickly turn round, then race off in the same direction as the ball.

Dan has the ball, but an opponent is closing in on him. Suddenly, Dan stops running. He steps over the ball, then stops it dead with his foot.

Dan pushes the ball behind him, then turns and sprints off in a different direction. The red **defender** is left wondering what has happened!

Feinting

Feinting is pretending that you are about to turn one way, then turning another. To fool an opponent, try glancing in the wrong direction, dropping your shoulder or twisting your body. Here's Liz in action…

1 Liz is dribbling up the field towards a red **defender** who is blocking her path. Notice the way she keeps the ball close to her feet — good work, Liz!

2 As she gets closer to the red player, Liz drops her right shoulder to make it look as though she is turning to her right. The defender falls for the trick.

3 Quick as a flash, Liz turns to her left, using the outside of her left foot to control the ball. The red player moves to his left, but Liz dodges past him and sprints away.

Inside hook

When there's a defender hot on your tail, try this move. Use the inside of one foot to hook the ball, while you turn on the heel of the other foot.

Raj leans slightly to one side. He stretches for the ball and hooks it with the inside of his right foot.

Raj makes a half turn on his left foot and speeds off in the other direction with the ball.

HOT TIPS
Never dribble in your own penalty area — it's too risky! Show off your skills in the midfield, or near the goal you are attacking.

IN TRAINING!

To test your dribbling skills, set up a row of traffic cones (or you could use jumpers) approximately two metres apart. Then practise dribbling the ball in and out of the obstacles.

Vary your pace by speeding up and slowing down. When you reach the last obstacle in the line, turn around and dribble the ball back to the beginning again.

11

Passing

66 **Passing** is vital for **midfielders** like me, but it's a skill that all players must learn. Passing the ball accurately between team-mates is the key to scoring goals. So pay attention and I'll show you how it's done! 99

▲ The England midfielder Jamie Redknapp begins another attack by passing the ball to Paul Scholes.

Short pass

If a team-mate nearby is in a better position than you, pass the ball! A short pass along the ground is easy. All you need to do is practise controlling the ball. One other thing — only use this type of pass if there is a clear path between you and your team-mate.

Raj places his non-kicking foot next to the ball and turns his body towards the target. Watch how he keeps his upper body and head over the ball.

Raj swings his leg and strikes the middle of the ball to keep the pass low. You can use the inside or outside of your foot for this shot.

Chip pass

A chip is a short pass that lifts the ball high into the air. Use this technique to pass to someone nearby when there's an opposition player in the way. With practice, you'll be able to pop the ball over your opponent's head so that it lands at your team-mate's feet.

Matt's non-kicking foot is beside the ball. With his other foot, he stabs down beneath the ball and follows the ball through for extra power.

Ben

Matt

Matt chips the ball to Ben, over the head of the opposition player.

HOT TIPS

Lean forwards for a short pass, but for a lofted pass, or a chip, lean backwards to make the ball go further.

Lofted pass

A lofted pass is a long, high pass. Defenders and midfielders use it to send the ball upfield. It's also a good pass to use when you take a corner. A lofted pass is more risky than a short pass because it's harder to control where the ball lands, especially on a windy day!

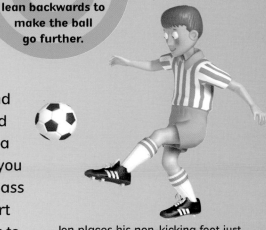

Jon places his non-kicking foot just behind and to the side of the ball. He strikes the bottom of the ball with his instep and follows through.

Jon clears the ball out of his own half and it reaches Dan in midfield. That's good defending, Jon!

Wall pass

The wall pass is also called the 'one-two'. It's a trick that two attacking players use to overcome a single defender. They pass the ball quickly between themselves.

1 Ben runs with the ball straight towards the defender. At the last moment, he passes the ball to Liz.

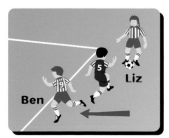

2 Ben keeps running past the defender into an open space. The defender follows the ball towards Liz.

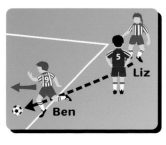

3 As soon as the ball reaches Liz, she taps it into the open space. Ben meets the ball and sprints towards the goal. Make sure you're **onside**, Ben!

IN TRAINING!

This drill helps to improve the timing and accuracy of your passing – you'll need a friend. Place five cones one metre apart on the ground.

Slowly dribble the ball around the outside of the cones. Pass the ball to your friend through a gap in the cones. Keep walking as your friend dribbles the ball and passes it back to you through another gap. Gradually speed up and try passing to each other while you jog.

Receiving the ball

❝ Now you've learned how to **pass** the ball, you need to know how to receive it. Let me show you how to use your feet, thighs and chest to cushion the ball so that it doesn't bounce away from you. **❞**

▲ Edgar Davids, the Juventus player, is a strong and skilful **midfielder**. Here he controls the ball on his chest.

Feet first

When the ball is rolling along the ground, you can stop it with your foot. This is the most straightforward way to receive the ball. Lift your foot slightly off the **pitch** and turn it sideways to meet the ball. As the ball hits your boot, draw back your foot to absorb the impact.

You can use either side of your foot. Here, Dan uses the inside of his foot to meet the middle of the ball.

As the ball reaches Dan, he draws his foot back. This stops the ball from bouncing off his boot.

In the air

If the ball is in the air, you can receive it with your thigh. Just as the ball lands, relax your leg muscles – this will take some of the power out of the ball's flight. The higher up your thigh the ball lands, the more easily you will be able to control it, so don't let it bounce off your knee!

Kim moves into position, keeping her eyes on the ball. She lifts up her arms to help her to balance.

As Kim makes contact with the ball, she brings her leg down gently. Easy does it, Kim – don't tense up!

Chest trap

Use your chest to control a high ball that's dropping down in front of you. Line yourself up to meet the ball and keep your hands out of the way — you don't want to give away a **hand-ball**! You can control the direction of the ball by twisting your body as the ball lands.

Kim faces the ball and pushes out her chest to meet it. She doesn't take her eyes off the ball for a second!

As the ball lands on Kim's chest, she lets her body sag back and go slack. The ball drops neatly to her feet!

What a catch!

You're not allowed to catch the ball with your hands, but you can try catching it with your feet! Use this skilful move to receive a ball in the air that's almost out of reach. You'll need to practise!

Dan stretches out his leg towards the ball, using his arms to balance. His toe points up and outwards.

HOT TIPS
To stop a ball that's rolling gently along the ground, place the sole of your foot on top of the ball and wedge it down.

Dan catches the ball perfectly in the curve of his instep and gently guides the ball to the ground.

IN TRAINING!

Here's an easy drill for practising ball control. Stand in front of a friend and ask him to throw or kick a ball to you. Ask him to vary the height and power of each pass without telling you what he is going to do.

Use your feet, thighs and chest to cushion the ball as it comes towards you. Try to make the ball land at your feet each time. If the ball bounces back to the thrower three times, swap over!

15

Heading

66 It's time to start using your head! Hitting the ball with your head is called **heading** the ball. It shouldn't hurt a bit, but if it does, you're not doing it properly! Try practising with a soft ball at first, to get used to it. 99

▲ The Scotland defender Colin Hendry jumps highest to head the ball clear of Sol Campbell of England.

Basic header

As the ball comes towards you, position yourself underneath it and keep your eyes open until the last second. Then strike the ball with the middle of your forehead. Thrust your head forwards using your neck muscles. Keep your mouth closed or you may bite your tongue!

Tom pulls back his neck and upper body as he prepares to head the ball. He keeps his eyes open so that he can time his move perfectly.

Tom hits the ball between his eyebrows and hairline. He sends the ball forwards by pushing with his neck muscles. That didn't hurt at all!

Defensive header

Defenders head the ball to keep it away from their goal. Often, two players go for the ball. Then, defenders jump to meet the ball first and thrust themselves forwards to head the ball with extra force. The more powerful the header, the further up the **pitch** the ball will travel.

Sue times her run-up carefully. She wants to make contact with the ball when she is at the highest point in her jump.

Sue jumps at exactly the right time and reaches the ball before a **striker** who's taller than her. Good timing is more important than being tall!

Attacking header

Accuracy is crucial when you're going for goal. You can control and change the direction of the ball by flicking or nodding your head just as you make contact. It can take a slight touch to send the ball into the goal. Again, timing is the key to success!

Ben moves into position to meet a powerful **corner kick**. This is a good chance to use his head to score!

As Ben touches the ball, he flicks his head towards the goal. Hopefully, the ball will go into the back of the net.

TOP TACTICS

Defenders need to head the ball high and far to clear it from the goalmouth. It also pays to know where your team-mates are.

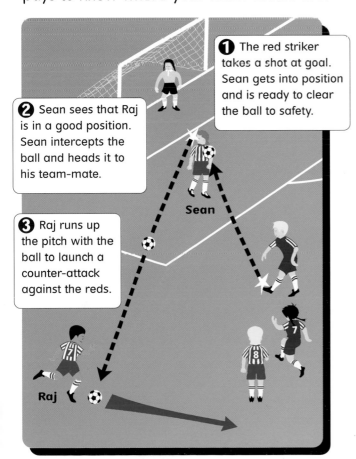

1 The red striker takes a shot at goal. Sean gets into position and is ready to clear the ball to safety.

2 Sean sees that Raj is in a good position. Sean intercepts the ball and heads it to his team-mate.

3 Raj runs up the pitch with the ball to launch a counter-attack against the reds.

Sean

Raj

IN TRAINING!

Ask a friend to stand behind the goal and chip or throw the ball over the crossbar – that's the bar that runs along the top of the goal. Your job is to try to score using your head.

When you've scored five goals, swap positions with your friend. Once you've got the hang of it, you could ask another friend to play goalie – that should make things a lot more difficult!

Shooting

" When you have a chance to score, take it! Stay calm and choose your target. Kick the ball hard and aim as far away from the **goalie** and the **defenders** as you can. Not every shot will go in, but the more you practise, the better you'll become! "

▲ Gabriel Battistuta of Fiorentina is a fearsome **striker** of the ball. He's very good at scoring with volleys.

Low driven shot

When you're going for a goal, aim to send the ball just inside one of the posts. If you're feeling more daring, try to drive the ball straight past the keeper's legs. Keep the ball low — any goalie will tell you that powerful, low balls are the most difficult ones to save.

Liz's non-kicking foot is beside the ball. Liz swings her kicking foot back behind her. She aims to kick the middle of the ball with her instep.

Liz strikes the ball well. She swings her leg all the way through, after the ball. This follow-through makes her shot extra powerful.

Swerve shot

The aim of this shot is to make the ball spin when you kick it so that it swerves as it flies through the air. This type of shot is often used for taking **direct free kicks** and **penalty kicks**. Once you've got the knack, it's deadly!

Ben wants to curve the ball to the right, so he aims for the left-hand side of the ball. He strikes it with the outside of the top of his boot.

As Ben's foot connects with the ball, the ball spins to the right. With a bit of luck, the ball will curve away from the keeper — straight into the goal!

IN TRAINING!

Accuracy is everything when it comes to shooting, so you'll need to practise. Use chalk to draw six squares on a wall and number them 1 to 6. at the squares, starting at 1.

Try to hit each square in turn. Then practise shooting at the squares from different distances and angles.

The wall

▼ This is Middlesbrough's Christian Ziege in action, swerving the ball around a '**wall**' of Southampton players in a Premiership match.

TOP TACTICS

A lot of work is needed to build an attacking move. This tactic shows how a team can work together to create a goal-scoring opportunity.

HOT TIPS

Be prepared for the ball to   , or bounce, off the keeper or the post. Go after the ball and follow up your shot!

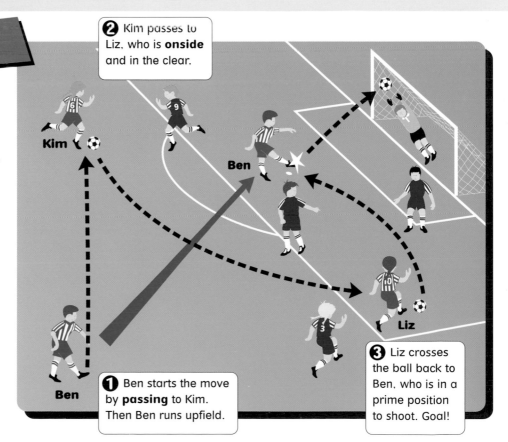

2 Kim passes to Liz, who is **onside** and in the clear.

Kim

Ben

1 Ben starts the move by **passing** to Kim. Then Ben runs upfield.

Ben

Liz

3 Liz crosses the ball back to Ben, who is in a prime position to shoot. Goal!

Defending

" When it comes to stopping the opposition from scoring, the whole team can help, not just the **defenders**! Everyone needs to be good at **tackling** and **marking** – two important defensive skills. Let me explain... **"**

▲ The England midfielder Rob Lee is in a defensive role here as he keeps the ball away from Llian Liev of Bulgaria.

Marking

There are two different ways of marking. You can mark an opponent, which means that wherever that player goes, you go too. Or you can mark part of the **pitch**, defending that part against any opposition player who enters it.

Sue marks her opponent by staying as close to him as possible. She can touch him, but she must not push or hold him. That would be a **foul**!

This time Sue marks part of the pitch. Notice how Sue stays between the goal and the red attacker. She watches him closely and blocks his path wherever he moves.

Basic tackle

To tackle well, you need lots of practice and confidence. You may only tackle when your opponent has the ball, and remember – kick the ball, not your opponent! Use the inside of your boot and try to push the ball behind your attacker.

Jon bends his knees and positions his body over the ball. He uses his bodyweight to help him push the ball over the red attacker's foot.

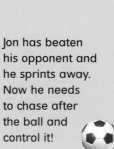

Jon has beaten his opponent and he sprints away. Now he needs to chase after the ball and control it!

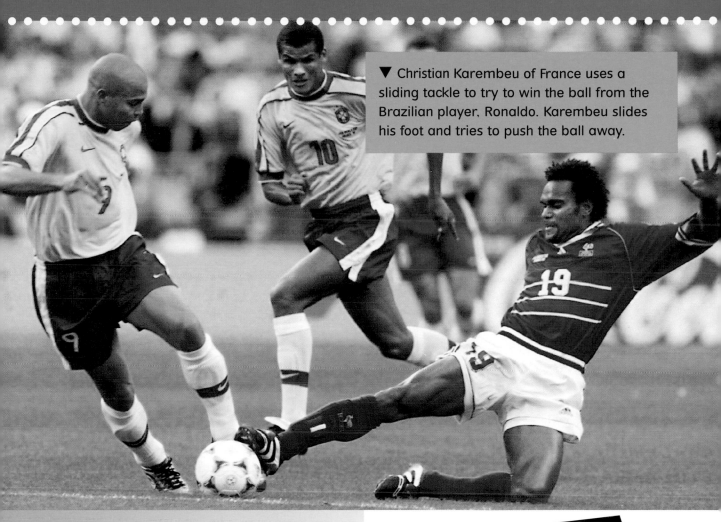

▼ Christian Karembeu of France uses a sliding tackle to try to win the ball from the Brazilian player, Ronaldo. Karembeu slides his foot and tries to push the ball away.

Blocking

When your opponent is about to **shoot**, try to **block** the path of the ball with your body. Be brave! Turn sideways and raise your leg to meet the ball. As soon as the ball bounces off you, be ready to race after it and regain possession.

Sue

Sue waits until the last moment to make her move. She wants to be sure that the red attacker will shoot.

Sue blocks the shot with her leg. Now she needs to watch where the ball goes and try to reach it first.

IN TRAINING!

Here's a drill that helps you to polish your tackling skills. All you need is a friend and two footballs. The idea is to protect your own ball while you tackle your opponent and try to steal his ball.

Every time you capture your opponent's ball, you win a point. Every time you lose your own ball, you lose a point. The first person to reach ten points is the winner!

Goalkeeping

" Goalkeepers often notice things that other players miss, which is why you often see us shouting out instructions. But a goalie's main job is to protect her own goal and to stop the other team from scoring. Here's how it's done... **"**

▲ Fabien Barthez, the goalkeeper for France, catches the ball, to stop Davor Suker of Croatia scoring.

Catching high shots

The goalie is the only player on the **pitch** who is allowed to touch the ball with her hands during play. Even then, she is only allowed to handle the ball inside her own goal area! If you are the goalie, try to catch the ball in front of your face and don't stretch for it unless you have to.

Julie positions herself in line with the ball. Her hands are held high and her thumbs are almost touching. Watch the ball, Julie!

As Julie catches the ball, she pulls it down towards her tummy. She bends over the ball to protect it with her body. Hold on tight!

Catching low shots

Low shots are the hardest to save. The trick is to move your whole body behind the ball, not just your hands. If you have time, bend down on one knee. Lean forwards so that you're ready to dive on top of the ball if it bounces away from you. Don't take your eyes off the ball!

An attacker sends a low ball Julie's way. Quick as a flash, she kneels down to stop the shot. Julie's palms face outwards to meet the ball.

As the ball reaches Julie, her leg is side-on to the ball. She cups both hands and scoops the ball up to her chest. Another great save!

Clearing the ball

You won't always be able to catch the ball with your hands. When you can't catch it, clear it! Punch the ball as hard as you can towards one of your **defenders**. If you can't punch the ball, try to knock it out of play, either by sending it over the **crossbar** or by tapping it over the goal line.

This ball is too high to catch, so Julie jumps in the air, reaches the ball and tips it over the top of the crossbar.

Julie dives to save the ball and just reaches it with her fingertips. She pushes it around the goalpost and across the goal line.

Narrowing the angle

A goalie faced with a single attacker should come out of the **goalmouth** towards the ball. This makes it more difficult for the **striker** to score.

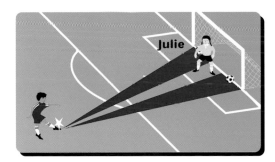

❶ Julie is standing too far back in goal. This shot isn't going to be easy to save – the red striker has a wide area to aim at!

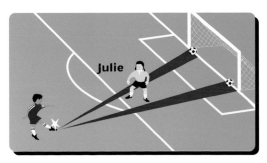

❷ This time, Julie comes forward. She puts the striker under pressure because he has less space to aim at. Nice work, Julie!

IN TRAINING!

If you like playing in goal, try this exercise. Stand in the middle of the goal. Ask four friends, each holding a ball, to stand in a row about three metres in front of you. Ask each friend to throw his or her ball in turn, so that it bounces just in front of your goal line. Your job is to stop each ball crossing the line.

If you think you can handle this, try turning your back to your friends. Now ask them to shout out as they throw the ball. Quickly turn around and try to stop the ball.

Dead ball

" When the **referee** blows his whistle, it means that the ball is 'dead' and play must stop immediately. There are lots of different ways to get the ball back in play. Here are several **dead-ball** skills you'll need to learn... **"**

▲ Gianfranco Zola, the Chelsea striker, swoops down on the ball to take a **corner kick**.

Throw-in

If one team knocks the ball over the touchline, the Ref awards a **throw-in** to the other team. Usually, the referee's assistant, called the linesman, decides where the ball crossed the line. The quicker you take a throw-in, the better – it keeps the opposition on their toes!

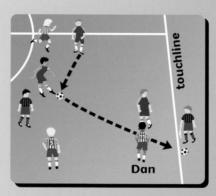

A red player knocks the ball over the touchline, so the blue team wins a throw-in. The linesman shows Dan where he should take it.

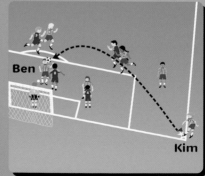

Dan stands behind the line with both feet on the ground. Dan leans back for extra power. He must throw the ball over his head with both hands.

Corner kick

When a player knocks the ball over his own goal line, the Ref gives a **corner kick** to the other team. This is a good chance to score! Often, the best kind of corner kick is a high ball that drops down into the goal area. Here, the attackers are at the ready to head the ball into goal.

Raj tries to pass the ball to Liz, but a red **defender** intercepts the ball and knocks it over his own goal line. The Ref awards a corner.

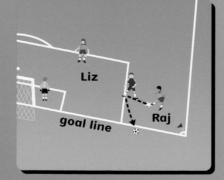

Kim takes the corner. She lofts the ball high in the air and it drops down towards Ben. It's Ben's job to head the ball into the goal. Go for it, Ben!

Goal kick

When a player knocks the ball over his opponent's goal line, the Ref awards a goal kick to the opponent's team. The kick may be taken from anywhere inside the goal area and by any player. While the kick is being taken, no opposition players are allowed in the goal area.

goal line

A red **striker** takes a shot at goal, but the ball sails just over the **crossbar** and crosses the goal line. It's a goal kick to the blues!

Julie

Julie takes a short run-up and sends a long, high ball upfield. The players on the halfway line run towards the ball and jump up to try and win it.

Penalty kick

When a player commits a serious **foul** inside his own penalty area, the Ref blows the whistle — it's a **penalty kick** to the other team. One player kicks the ball from the penalty spot and tries to score. During this shot all other players must stay outside the penalty area and penalty arc.

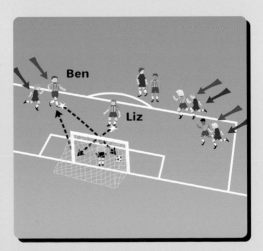

Ben

Liz

Liz takes the penalty. She takes a short run-up and kicks a low ball towards the goal corner. As she kicks the ball, the other players run forwards. The ball hits the post and rebounds towards Ben, who scores!

TOP TACTICS

The referee has awarded a **direct free kick** to the blue team, just outside the penalty area. This means that they can **shoot** straight at goal. The red players form a **wall** in front of the goal to **block** the shot, but the blue team has a plan...

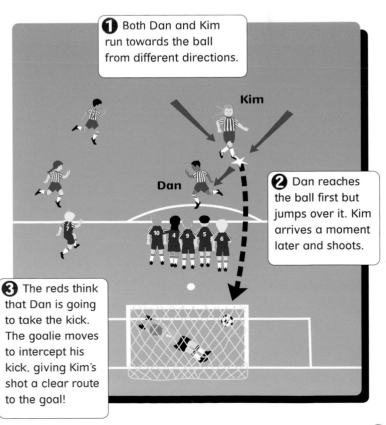

1 Both Dan and Kim run towards the ball from different directions.

Kim

Dan

2 Dan reaches the ball first but jumps over it. Kim arrives a moment later and shoots.

3 The reds think that Dan is going to take the kick. The goalie moves to intercept his kick, giving Kim's shot a clear route to the goal!

25

Advanced play

66 Once you've got to grips with the basic tactics, you can start learning more advanced **soccer** skills. These moves take a lot of practice, as you are about to discover! Perfecting them is what makes a football player into a football hero. **99**

▲ Manchester United's Henning Berg throws himself forward to meet the ball with a dynamic diving header.

Volley shot

Kicking the ball while it's in the air is called volleying. If you're a **striker**, it's a useful skill to master. Don't wait for the ball to bounce — kick it in midair, just before it lands. The **goalie** and the **defenders** will have less time to prepare.

Ben keeps his body and kicking knee over the ball to stop it rising. Ben's toes are pointed down to keep the ball low.

Diving header

For this header, you launch yourself at the ball to give your header extra power. Timing is everything. Get it wrong and you may dive nose-first into the **pitch**!

The ball comes towards Raj below head height. Raj pushes with his left leg and hurls himself at the ball.

Side volley

To perform this tricky variation on the volley, stand sideways to the ball. As the ball approaches, pivot on one leg and swing up your kicking foot. Keep your eye on the ball, lean back and use your arms to help you to balance.

Ben keeps his head forwards, even though he is leaning back. This helps to keep his shot low.

Raj performs a brilliant diving header. He flicks his head sideways towards the goal and spreads out his arms to break his fall.

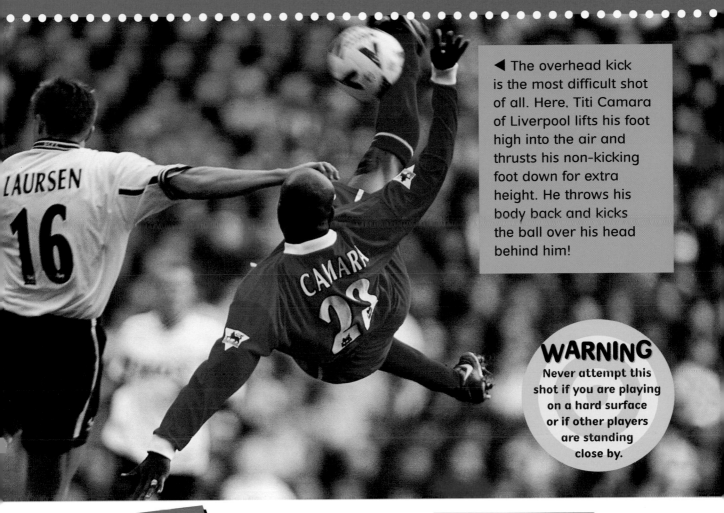

◀ The overhead kick is the most difficult shot of all. Here, Titi Camara of Liverpool lifts his foot high into the air and thrusts his non-kicking foot down for extra height. He throws his body back and kicks the ball over his head behind him!

WARNING
Never attempt this shot if you are playing on a hard surface or if other players are standing close by.

TOP TACTICS

Use the size of the **pitch** to your advantage. Here, the blue team creates space to attack by **passing** the ball out wide, to the edge of the pitch.

HOT TIPS
Remember your ABC – Accuracy, Balance and Control! And never use a difficult shot if a simple one will do.

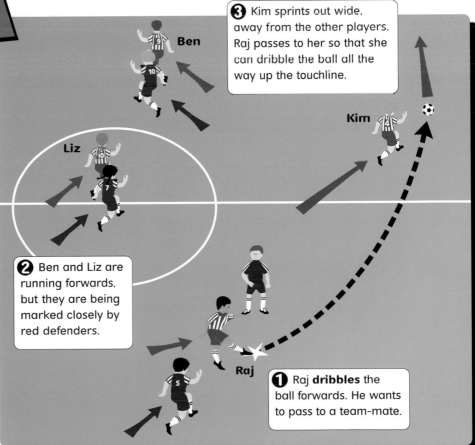

❸ Kim sprints out wide, away from the other players. Raj passes to her so that she can dribble the ball all the way up the touchline.

Ben

Kim

Liz

❷ Ben and Liz are running forwards, but they are being marked closely by red defenders.

Raj

❶ Raj **dribbles** the ball forwards. He wants to pass to a team-mate.

Hall of Fame

" Every once in a while, an amazing footballer comes along. He may be a goal-scorer, he may bring his country to **World Cup** victory, but one thing is sure, he must have talent. This is my list of the top five most talented players of all time. See if you agree. "

PELE

Name Edson Arantes do Nascimento — but known to football fans everywhere as Pele!
Date of birth 21 October 1940
Country Brazil

Did you know? Pele is the youngest player ever to have received a World Cup winner's medal. He scored two goals in the 1958 final, when Brazil defeated Sweden 5-2.
Achievements Pele is the greatest player the world has ever seen. He helped Brazil to win the World Cup three times. During his career, Pele played in 1,363 professional matches, scoring a record 1,281 goals!

HOT SHOTS
Brazil holds the World Cup record. The team has won the trophy an incredible four times! The last time was in 1994.

BECKENBAUER

Name Franz Beckenbauer
Date of birth 11 September 1945
Country Germany

Did you know? Beckenbauer worked as an insurance salesman before he played professional football.
Achievements Beckenbauer played for West Germany's World Cup team in 1966 and 1970, and was captain when the team won in 1974. After making 103 appearances for his country, Beckenbauer retired. In 1984, he returned to the West German team as manager. Six years later, in 1990, he guided his players to another World Cup victory!

MARADONA

Name Diego Maradona
Date of birth 3 October 1960
Country Argentina

Did you know? Maradona's second goal against England in Mexico in 1986 was voted the greatest World Cup goal ever. He started the move in his own half, then dribbled past half of the England team before scoring.
Achievements Maradona was only 16 when he first played for Argentina. He captained the team to the finals of the 1986 and 1990 World Cup tournaments. In 1986, Argentina won and Maradona was voted Player of the Tournament.

EUSEBIO

Name Eusebio Da Silva Ferreira — but known simply as Eusebio!
Date of birth 25 January 1942
Country Portugal

Did you know? A statue of Eusebio stands in his honour outside his old club, Benfica, in Lisbon, Portugal.
Achievements Eusebio helped Benfica win the Portuguese League seven times and the Portuguese Cup five times. He played for Portugal 46 times and scored 38 goals, nine of them during the 1966 World Cup.

GEORGE BEST

Name George Best
Date of birth 22 May 1946
Country Northern Ireland

Did you know? Before Best signed with Manchester United, several teams rejected him. They thought he was too skinny and weak!
Achievements Pele said that Best was the most talented player he had ever seen. Best helped Man Utd win the European Cup in 1968, when he was named European Footballer of the Year. In an FA Cup game in 1970, Best scored six goals! This record still stands today.

Football phrases

blocking Using your body or leg to stop the ball when your opponent takes a shot at goal.

booking When the referee gives a player a formal warning by showing the yellow card.

corner kick When a defender kicks or deflects the ball over his own goal line, an attacker restarts the game by kicking the ball from the corner closest to where the ball crossed the goal line.

crossbar The horizontal bar that lies across the top of the goalposts.

dead ball A ball that has gone out of play.

defender A playing position, or a player who is part of the defensive team.

deflection A ball that has bounced off either the goalpost, crossbar or another player.

direct free kick A free kick in which the player taking the kick may aim directly for the goal and score, without anyone else touching the ball.

dribbling Running with the ball using the insides and outsides of your feet to tap it forwards and keep it under control.

FA Cup The FA stands for Football Association. The FA organised the world's first-ever football competition. The first FA Cup final took place in 1872.

FIFA This stands for the Fédération Internationale de Football Association. FIFA was created in Switzerland in 1904. FIFA is responsible for deciding the rules of the game and organising international football competitions, such as the World Cup.

formation Before a game, the coach decides where to place each member of the team on the pitch. Depending on the formation he chooses, he can make the team more attacking or more defensive.

foul To break one of the rules of football. A foul is sometimes called a violation.

free kick When the Ref gives a player a chance to kick the ball, without interference from the other team.

goalkeeper A playing position, or the player who guards her team's goal. This player is also called the goalie, or keeper. A goalie is the only player who can touch the ball with her hands when the ball is in play.

goal kick A kick taken by either the goalie or a defender in their own goal area. A goal kick restarts the game after an attacking team has sent the ball over a defensive team's goal line.

goalmouth The area directly in front of the goal.

half-time A short break in the middle of the match (after 45 minutes), so that players can rest and discuss tactics. When play resumes, the two teams swap ends.

hand-ball It is a foul for a player other than the goalie to touch the ball with his hands. If this happens, the Ref awards a free kick to the other team.

heading Using your head to hit the ball.

indirect free kick A free kick in which the ball must touch another player before a goal can be scored.

kick-off Each half of the game begins with a player kicking the ball from the centre spot. The ball is also kicked from here after a goal has been scored.

marking Guarding an opponent to prevent him from getting the ball, or guarding an area of the pitch.

midfielder A playing position, or a player who runs upfield to attack, or downfield to defend, depending on how she is needed. Sometimes, midfielders are called halfbacks.

obstruction Deliberately getting in the way of an opponent and stopping him from getting the ball without trying to play the ball yourself. This is a foul!

offside When a team-mate behind you passes the ball forwards, there must be at least two opponents level with or between you and the goal. If not, you're offside.

onside Having at least two opponents level with or between you and the goal when the ball is played forwards.

passing Sending the ball to a team-mate without using the hands or arms.

penalty kick When a defending team commits a foul in its own penalty area, an attacking player kicks the ball from the penalty spot.

pitch A football pitch must be 90-120 metres long, and 45-90 metres wide. The touchline must always be longer than the goal line. Junior footballers play on smaller pitches.

referee The referee, or Ref, is in charge of the game. He makes sure that both teams play by the rules. The Ref also stops and starts the game.

shoot To try to score by kicking the ball at your opponent's goal.

soccer The word soccer is short for 'association football', which is the official name of the game.

striker A playing position, or a player who spends most of her time in the attacking half of the pitch trying to score a goal.

tackling Using your feet to take the ball away from an opponent.

throw-in When a player kicks the ball over the touchline, a player from the other team throws the ball back into play. The player must hold the ball in both hands and throw it over his head, while keeping both feet on the ground.

wall A defensive barrier formed when several members of a team stand next to each other in order to block a free kick.

World Cup An international competition that was first held in 1930 and which has been held every four years since — except during World War II.

Index

Help!

So you want to know more about playing football with a local team? Here are a few hot tips…

● First try getting involved with your school team.

● Check out your local park. Teams often play at the weekends. Why not ask if you can join in?

● The Football Association can give you a list of clubs in your area.

● Contact your local club and ask for the Football in the Community department. Someone there will explain how you can become involved in after-school and Saturday morning training sessions at your local football ground.

● Go to as many training sessions as possible and watch out for trial dates. With dedication you may join a local youth team. Good luck!

Useful addresses

The Football Association
16 Lancaster Gate
London W2 3LW
Tel: 020 7 262 4542

FIFA
PO Box 85
Zurich 8030
Switzerland
Tel: 004 113 849 595

Check out these websites:
www.soccer-sites.com
www.soccerclinics.com
www.reddingcal.com/ISKA/ISKA.ht